CONTENTS

Lesson 1: Overview of Microgreens	1
History and Evolution of Microgreens	3
The Growing Popularity of Microgreens in Modern Diets	5
Why Start a Microgreens Business?	7
Conducting Market Research	9
Identifying Your Target Market	11
Creating a Business Plan	13
Business Licensing and Permits	15
Food Safety Regulations	17
Setting Up Your Business Structure	20
Cost Breakdown	22
Setting Up Your Microgreens Farm	24
Essential Equipment and Supplies	27
Growing Microgreens	30
Marketing and Selling Microgreens	33
Scaling Up Your Microgreens Business	36
Case Studies and Success Stories in Microgreens Business	39
Future Trends and Opportunities in Microgreens Business	42
Resources and Tools for Microgreens Business	45
Your Journey in Microgreens	48
Case Study 1: Hamama	50

Case Study 2: The Chef's Garden	51
Case Study 3: Tiny Greens	52
Case Study 4: City Roots	53
Key Takeaways from Case Studies:	54
Additional Resources:	55
1. Radish Microgreens	56
2. Sunflower Microgreens	57
3. Pea Shoots	58
4. Broccoli Microgreens	59
5. Basil Microgreens	60
6. Arugula Microgreens	61
7. Cilantro Microgreens	62
8. Kale Microgreens	63
9. Mustard Microgreens	64
10. Beet Microgreens	65
11. Swiss Chard Microgreens	66
12. Spinach Microgreens	67
13. Amaranth Microgreens	68
14. Fenugreek Microgreens	69
15. Wheatgrass	70
Important Considerations for Business:	71
A sample list of some common microgreens varieties and their uses:	72

LESSON 1: OVERVIEW OF MICROGREENS

What are Microgreens?

Microgreens are young vegetable greens that are harvested at an early stage of growth, typically when the first true leaves have developed. They are smaller than baby greens and larger than sprouts, offering a unique blend of flavors, textures, and colors.

Characteristics of Microgreens:

1. **Nutrient Density:** Despite their small size, microgreens are packed with nutrients, including vitamins, minerals, and antioxidants.
2. **Quick Growth:** Microgreens have a rapid growth cycle, usually ready for harvest within 1-3 weeks after germination.
3. **Versatility:** They come in a variety of flavors, ranging from mild and sweet to spicy and tangy, making them versatile ingredients in culinary dishes.
4. **Colorful Appearance:** Microgreens exhibit vibrant colors, adding visual appeal to salads, sandwiches, and other dishes.
5. **Easy to Grow:** Microgreens can be grown indoors year-round with minimal space and equipment, making them accessible to home gardeners and commercial growers alike.

Importance of Microgreens:

- **Nutritional Benefits:** Microgreens are densely packed with vitamins, minerals, and antioxidants, making them

a valuable addition to a healthy diet.
- **Culinary Use:** Chefs around the world use microgreens to enhance the flavor, texture, and visual presentation of their dishes.
- **Sustainable Agriculture:** Microgreens can be grown sustainably using hydroponic or soil-based methods, requiring less water and space compared to traditional crops.
- **Market Demand:** The growing interest in healthy eating and gourmet cuisine has fueled the demand for microgreens in both consumer and commercial markets.

Understanding the basics of microgreens is essential for anyone interested in starting a microgreens business or incorporating them into their culinary repertoire. Their nutrient density, versatility, and ease of cultivation make them a valuable asset in modern agriculture and gastronomy.

HISTORY AND EVOLUTION OF MICROGREENS

Ancient Origins:
- **Early Cultivation:** Microgreens have been cultivated for thousands of years, with evidence of their consumption dating back to ancient civilizations such as the Egyptians, Greeks, and Romans.
- **Medicinal Use:** In traditional medicine, young plants were prized for their medicinal properties and used to treat various ailments.

Modern Revival:
- **Research and Innovation:** In the 1980s, researchers began studying the nutritional profiles of young plants, leading to the discovery of the concentrated nutrients found in microgreens.
- **Chefs' Interest:** Chefs and culinary experts recognized the potential of microgreens as flavor-packed garnishes and salad ingredients, sparking a trend in fine dining establishments.

Commercial Adoption:
- **Commercial Production:** In the 1990s, commercial growers started cultivating microgreens on a larger scale to meet the increasing demand from restaurants, specialty food markets, and health-conscious consumers.

- **Market Expansion:** Microgreens quickly gained popularity beyond gourmet restaurants, becoming staple ingredients in home kitchens and mainstream grocery stores.

Technological Advances:
- **Hydroponic Systems:** Advancements in hydroponic farming technology made it easier to grow microgreens indoors, year-round, without the need for soil.
- **Vertical Farming:** Vertical farming techniques allowed growers to maximize space and efficiency, further expanding the availability of microgreens in urban areas.

Current Trends:
- **Health and Wellness:** Microgreens are recognized for their nutritional density and health benefits, aligning with the growing emphasis on healthy eating and plant-based diets.
- **Sustainable Agriculture:** Microgreens are cultivated using sustainable farming practices, making them an eco-friendly option for environmentally conscious consumers.
- **Innovation and Experimentation:** Growers continue to experiment with new varieties of microgreens and innovative growing techniques, pushing the boundaries of what is possible in microgreen production.

The history of microgreens is a testament to their resilience and adaptability, evolving from ancient medicinal herbs to modern-day culinary delicacies. Their journey from obscurity to mainstream popularity reflects changing trends in agriculture, cuisine, and consumer preferences.

THE GROWING POPULARITY OF MICROGREENS IN MODERN DIETS

Nutritional Powerhouses:
- **Concentrated Nutrients:** Microgreens are packed with vitamins, minerals, and antioxidants, often containing higher levels than their mature counterparts.
- **Diverse Nutritional Profiles:** Different varieties of microgreens offer unique nutritional compositions, providing a wide range of health benefits.
- **Bioavailability:** The young and tender leaves of microgreens are easily digestible, allowing for optimal nutrient absorption.

Culinary Versatility:
- **Flavor Enhancement:** Microgreens add a burst of fresh flavors and textures to dishes, enhancing the overall taste and aesthetic appeal.
- **Garnishes and Toppings:** They are commonly used as garnishes on soups, salads, sandwiches, and main courses, adding color and freshness.
- **Creative Ingredient:** Chefs and home cooks alike use microgreens creatively in various recipes, from simple salads to gourmet entrees.

Health and Wellness Benefits:
- **Nutrient Density:** Microgreens offer a concentrated source of essential nutrients, supporting overall health and vitality.
- **Antioxidant Properties:** The abundance of antioxidants in microgreens helps combat oxidative stress and reduce the risk of chronic diseases.
- **Weight Management:** Incorporating microgreens into meals can aid in weight management by adding volume and flavor without excess calories.

Culinary Trends and Consumer Preferences:
- **Gourmet Cuisine:** Microgreens have become a staple in gourmet restaurants, featured prominently in chef-driven dishes and culinary creations.
- **Healthy Eating Movement:** The growing emphasis on health-conscious eating has propelled the popularity of microgreens among consumers seeking nutritious and wholesome foods.
- **Plant-Based Diets:** Microgreens are favored by individuals following plant-based diets, providing a nutrient-rich alternative to animal products.

Accessibility and Availability:
- **Home Cultivation:** With the rise of indoor gardening and hydroponic systems, microgreens are increasingly cultivated at home by gardening enthusiasts and health-conscious individuals.
- **Supermarket Staples:** Microgreens are now commonly found in supermarkets and specialty food stores, offering convenient access to consumers nationwide.

WHY START A MICROGREENS BUSINESS?

Low Startup Costs and Quick Turnaround:
- **Minimal Investment:** Compared to traditional farming ventures, starting a microgreens business requires relatively low startup costs, making it accessible to aspiring entrepreneurs with limited capital.
- **Affordable Equipment:** Basic equipment such as trays, seeds, and grow lights can be purchased at a relatively low cost, allowing entrepreneurs to set up their operations quickly and affordably.
- **Fast Growth Cycle:** Microgreens have a rapid growth cycle, typically ready for harvest within 1-3 weeks, allowing for quick turnaround and a steady stream of revenue.

High Market Demand and Profitability:
- **Increasing Consumer Interest:** The growing interest in healthy eating and gourmet cuisine has fueled the demand for microgreens among health-conscious consumers, restaurants, and specialty food markets.
- **Premium Pricing:** Microgreens command premium prices due to their nutritional density, fresh flavors, and vibrant colors, resulting in higher profit margins for growers.
- **Steady Demand:** Microgreens have a year-round market

demand, providing a consistent source of income for growers regardless of seasonality or weather conditions.

Opportunities for Innovation and Growth:
- **Diverse Product Range:** Microgreens offer a wide variety of options for growers to experiment with, including different varieties, flavors, and growing techniques, allowing for creativity and innovation.
- **Value-Added Products:** Beyond fresh produce, growers can expand their product offerings to include value-added products such as microgreen kits, infused oils, and salad mixes, diversifying revenue streams and attracting new customers.

CONDUCTING MARKET RESEARCH

Identifying Target Demographics:
- **Definition:** Target demographics refer to the specific groups of people who are most likely to be interested in your product or service. For a microgreens business, this may include health-conscious consumers, gourmet chefs, urban dwellers, or individuals following plant-based diets.
- **Research Methods:** Conduct surveys, interviews, or focus groups to gather information about your target demographics' preferences, behaviors, and purchasing habits.
- **Example:** If your target demographic consists of health-conscious consumers, you may focus on promoting the nutritional benefits and organic farming practices of your microgreens.

Analyzing Market Trends and Competitors:
- **Market Trends:** Research current trends in the microgreens industry, including popular varieties, growing techniques, and consumer preferences. Stay updated on emerging trends and innovations to identify opportunities for differentiation and growth.
- **Competitor Analysis:** Identify key competitors in the microgreens market, both locally and nationally. Analyze their products, pricing strategies, marketing efforts, and customer reviews to understand their strengths and

weaknesses.

- **Example:** If you notice a growing demand for organic microgreens in your area but limited availability, you may consider positioning your business as a provider of premium organic microgreens to capitalize on this trend.

Assessing Demand in Your Area:

- **Local Market Assessment:** Evaluate the demand for microgreens in your target area by exploring local farmers' markets, grocery stores, restaurants, and health food stores. Observe consumer behavior, ask questions, and gather feedback to gauge interest and demand.
- **Online Research:** Use online tools and resources, such as Google Trends, social media platforms, and industry reports, to gather data on microgreens consumption trends, search volume, and market dynamics in your region.
- **Example:** If you find that there is limited availability of microgreens in your area but a growing interest from consumers and chefs, there may be a significant opportunity to fill this gap and meet unmet demand with your business.

IDENTIFYING YOUR TARGET MARKET

Defining Your Ideal Customers:
- **Understanding Customer Needs:** Start by identifying the types of customers who are most likely to benefit from and be interested in your microgreens products. This could include:
  - **Restaurants:** Chefs and restaurant owners seeking fresh, high-quality ingredients for their dishes.
  - **Health-Conscious Consumers:** Individuals who prioritize health and nutrition and are willing to pay a premium for fresh, nutrient-rich foods.
  - **Home Cooks:** Amateur chefs and cooking enthusiasts looking to elevate their culinary creations with gourmet ingredients.

Segmenting Your Market:
- **Market Segmentation:** Divide your target market into smaller, more manageable segments based on shared characteristics, preferences, and behaviors. This allows you to tailor your marketing efforts to specific customer groups.
- **Examples of Market Segments:**
  - **Demographic Segmentation:** Age, gender, income level, occupation.
  - **Psychographic Segmentation:** Lifestyle, values, interests, personality traits.

- **Behavioral Segmentation:** Buying habits, usage patterns, brand loyalty.
- **Tailored Marketing Strategies:** Develop marketing strategies and messaging that resonate with each market segment's unique needs and preferences. This could involve:
  - **Customized Messaging:** Craft marketing materials, such as advertisements, social media posts, and email campaigns, that speak directly to the interests and concerns of each segment.
  - **Targeted Promotions:** Offer special promotions, discounts, or incentives tailored to the preferences and buying behaviors of different customer groups.
  - **Personalized Customer Experiences:** Provide personalized customer service and experiences that make each segment feel valued and understood.

Example:

- **Segmentation Example:** Suppose you've identified two primary market segments for your microgreens business: health-conscious consumers and restaurants.
  - **Health-Conscious Consumers:** Focus on highlighting the nutritional benefits, freshness, and organic farming practices of your microgreens to appeal to this segment's desire for healthy, wholesome foods.
  - **Restaurants:** Emphasize the flavor, quality, and consistency of your microgreens to attract chefs and restaurant owners who value premium ingredients for their culinary creations.

CREATING A BUSINESS PLAN

Setting Clear Business Goals:
- **Define Your Objectives:** Start by identifying the overarching goals and objectives of your microgreens business. These may include:
  - **Revenue Targets:** Setting specific revenue goals for the business, such as annual sales targets or growth projections.
  - **Market Expansion:** Expanding into new markets or geographic regions to increase market share and reach a wider audience.
  - **Product Development:** Introducing new product lines or varieties of microgreens to meet evolving customer needs and preferences.

Outlining Operational Plans and Strategies:
- **Operational Plans:** Develop detailed plans for how you will operate and manage your microgreens business on a day-to-day basis. This may include:
  - **Production Processes:** Outlining the steps involved in growing, harvesting, and packaging microgreens, as well as quality control measures.
  - **Supply Chain Management:** Identifying suppliers for seeds, growing mediums, and other materials, as well as establishing efficient logistics and distribution channels.
  - **Quality Assurance:** Implementing protocols and

procedures to ensure the consistent quality and freshness of your microgreens.

Financial Projections and Funding Requirements:

- **Financial Projections:** Create realistic financial projections for your microgreens business, including revenue forecasts, expenses, and profit margins. Consider factors such as:
    - **Startup Costs:** Estimating the initial investment required to start and launch your microgreens business, including equipment, supplies, and marketing expenses.
    - **Operating Expenses:** Calculating ongoing expenses such as rent, utilities, labor costs, and packaging materials.
    - **Revenue Streams:** Identifying potential revenue streams, such as direct sales to consumers, wholesale distribution to restaurants and retailers, or value-added products.
- **Funding Requirements:** Determine how much funding you will need to start and sustain your microgreens business. Explore funding options such as:
    - **Self-Funding:** Investing your own savings or personal funds into the business.
    - **Loans and Financing:** Seeking loans from banks or financial institutions, or exploring alternative financing options such as crowdfunding or peer-to-peer lending.
    - **Investors:** Attracting investors or venture capitalists who are willing to provide funding in exchange for equity or ownership stakes in the business.

BUSINESS LICENSING AND PERMITS

Types of Business Licenses Required:
- **General Business License:** Most jurisdictions require businesses to obtain a general business license, also known as a business tax certificate or occupational license. This license allows you to operate legally within your jurisdiction and is typically issued by the local government.
- **Food Handling Permit:** If you are involved in the production, processing, or sale of food products like microgreens, you will likely need a food handling permit or license. This ensures that you comply with food safety regulations and maintain proper hygiene standards in your operations.

Local and State Regulations for Food Production:
- **Food Safety Regulations:** Microgreens are considered a food product and are subject to food safety regulations at both the local and state levels. These regulations govern various aspects of food production, including:
  - **Sanitation:** Maintaining clean and hygienic facilities, equipment, and utensils to prevent contamination.
  - **Storage and Handling:** Proper storage and handling of microgreens to minimize the risk of spoilage or foodborne illness.
  - **Labeling Requirements:** Providing accurate and

informative labels on packaging to ensure consumer safety and compliance with labeling regulations.
- **Permitting Process:** The permitting process for food production businesses may vary depending on your location and the scale of your operations. It typically involves:
    - **Application:** Submitting an application for a food handling permit to the appropriate regulatory authority, such as the local health department or department of agriculture.
    - **Inspections:** Undergoing inspections of your facilities and operations to ensure compliance with food safety regulations.
    - **Renewal:** Renewing your food handling permit annually or as required by local regulations to maintain legal compliance.

Example:
- **Local Regulations Example:** Suppose you are starting a microgreens business in a city that requires all food production businesses to obtain a food handling permit from the local health department. You would need to:
    - **Apply:** Submit an application for a food handling permit, providing details about your business operations and facilities.
    - **Inspection:** Schedule an inspection of your growing and processing facilities to ensure they meet the required health and safety standards.
    - **Compliance:** Make any necessary adjustments or improvements to your operations based on the inspection findings to ensure compliance with local regulations.

FOOD SAFETY REGULATIONS

Understanding HACCP (Hazard Analysis Critical Control Point):
- **Definition:** HACCP is a systematic approach to identifying, evaluating, and controlling food safety hazards throughout the production process. It focuses on critical control points (CCPs) where hazards can be prevented, eliminated, or reduced to acceptable levels.
- **Principles of HACCP:**
    1. **Conduct Hazard Analysis:** Identify potential hazards associated with microgreens production, such as biological, chemical, and physical hazards.
    2. **Identify Critical Control Points (CCPs):** Determine the points in the production process where control measures can be applied to prevent, eliminate, or reduce hazards to acceptable levels.
    3. **Establish Critical Limits:** Set measurable criteria for each CCP to ensure that hazards are effectively controlled.
    4. **Monitor CCPs:** Implement monitoring procedures to ensure that CCPs are operating within established critical limits.
    5. **Take Corrective Actions:** Develop procedures for taking corrective actions when CCPs deviate from critical limits to prevent unsafe products

from reaching consumers.
6. **Verify and Validate:** Verify that the HACCP plan is effective through regular inspections, testing, and validation of control measures.
7. **Documentation and Record-Keeping:** Maintain detailed records of HACCP plans, monitoring activities, corrective actions, and verification procedures for regulatory compliance and traceability.

Implementing Good Agricultural Practices (GAP):
- **Definition:** Good Agricultural Practices (GAP) are guidelines and standards designed to minimize the risk of contamination and ensure the safety and quality of agricultural products.
- **Key Practices of GAP for Microgreens Production:**
    - **Hygiene Practices:** Implement strict hygiene practices, including handwashing, sanitization of equipment and facilities, and wearing protective clothing to prevent contamination.
    - **Water Quality Management:** Use clean, potable water for irrigation and avoid potential sources of water contamination, such as untreated or polluted water sources.
    - **Soil and Growing Medium:** Ensure the use of clean, uncontaminated soil or growing medium for microgreens production, and regularly monitor soil quality to prevent contamination.
    - **Pest and Disease Management:** Implement integrated pest management (IPM) practices to control pests and diseases using environmentally sustainable methods, such as biological control and crop rotation.
    - **Harvest and Post-Harvest Handling:** Use clean,

sanitized harvesting tools and containers, and implement proper post-harvest handling practices to minimize the risk of contamination during storage and transportation.

SETTING UP YOUR BUSINESS STRUCTURE

Choosing a Business Entity:
- **Sole Proprietorship:** A sole proprietorship is the simplest form of business ownership, where the business is owned and operated by one individual. This structure offers simplicity and flexibility but does not provide personal liability protection.
- **Limited Liability Company (LLC):** An LLC is a popular choice for small businesses, offering personal liability protection for owners while allowing flexibility in management and taxation. It combines the benefits of a corporation with the simplicity of a partnership.
- **Partnership:** A partnership is a business owned and operated by two or more individuals. Partnerships can be general partnerships, where all partners share equally in profits and liabilities, or limited partnerships, where one or more partners have limited liability.
- **Corporation:** A corporation is a separate legal entity owned by shareholders. It provides limited liability protection for owners but involves more complex management and regulatory requirements.

Registering Your Business Name:
- **Choose a Name:** Select a unique and memorable name for your microgreens business that reflects your brand identity and resonates with your target market.
- **Check Availability:** Before registering your business

name, conduct a search to ensure that the name is not already in use by another business in your industry or geographic area.
- **Register the Name:** Once you have chosen a name that is available, register it with the appropriate government agency in your jurisdiction. This may involve registering with the state government, county clerk's office, or Secretary of State's office, depending on your location and business structure.
- **Consider Trademark Protection:** If you want to protect your business name from unauthorized use by competitors, consider applying for trademark protection through the United States Patent and Trademark Office (USPTO).

Example:
- **Business Structure Example:** Suppose you are starting a microgreens business called "Green Haven Microgreens" as a sole proprietorship. You would:
  - **Choose Business Entity:** Decide to operate as a sole proprietorship for simplicity and flexibility.
  - **Register Business Name:** Check the availability of the business name "Green Haven Microgreens" and register it with the appropriate government agency, such as the county clerk's office or Secretary of State's office.

COST BREAKDOWN

Initial Setup Costs:
- **Seeds:** The cost of seeds will vary depending on the variety and quantity purchased. It's essential to research suppliers and compare prices to ensure you're getting the best value for your money.
- **Trays:** Invest in high-quality trays that are durable and suitable for growing microgreens. Consider factors such as size, material, and drainage capabilities when selecting trays.
- **Lights:** Proper lighting is crucial for successful microgreens production. Invest in full-spectrum LED grow lights or fluorescent lights to provide the right amount of light for optimal growth.

Ongoing Operational Costs:
- **Utilities:** Factor in the cost of utilities such as electricity and water used for growing microgreens. LED grow lights are energy-efficient, but they still contribute to electricity costs, especially if used for extended periods.
- **Supplies:** Ongoing supplies include growing mediums, such as soil or hydroponic solutions, as well as packaging materials, such as containers and labels. Budget for these recurring expenses to ensure smooth operations.

Example Cost Breakdown:
- **Initial Setup Costs:**
    - Seeds: $100 (for various varieties)
    - Trays: $50 (for 20 durable trays)
    - Lights: $200 (for LED grow lights)

- Total: $350
- **Ongoing Operational Costs (Monthly):**
  - Utilities: $50 (electricity and water)
  - Supplies: $100 (growing mediums, packaging)
  - Total: $150

SETTING UP YOUR MICROGREENS FARM

Choosing the Right Location:
- **Accessibility:** Select a location that is easily accessible for transportation of supplies and distribution of products. Consider proximity to markets, suppliers, and potential customers.
- **Utilities:** Ensure access to essential utilities such as water and electricity, as well as drainage systems to manage excess water.
- **Zoning Regulations:** Check local zoning regulations and land use restrictions to ensure compliance with agricultural activities. Obtain any necessary permits or licenses for operating a microgreens farm in the chosen location.

Space Requirements:
- **Growing Area:** Determine the amount of space needed for growing microgreens based on projected production volume and crop rotation schedules.
- **Processing Area:** Allocate space for washing, packaging, and storing harvested microgreens, as well as any additional processing or value-added activities.
- **Storage Facilities:** Consider storage needs for seeds, growing supplies, packaging materials, and finished products.

Indoor vs. Outdoor Growing:
- **Indoor Growing:** Indoor growing offers greater control

over environmental conditions such as temperature, humidity, and lighting, allowing for year-round production and consistent crop quality. It requires investment in climate control systems, lighting, and growing racks or shelves.
- **Outdoor Growing:** Outdoor growing may be more cost-effective initially, as it relies on natural sunlight and ventilation. However, it is limited by seasonal changes in weather and may be susceptible to pests and environmental factors beyond control.

Climate and Environmental Controls:
- **Temperature:** Maintain optimal temperature conditions for microgreens growth, typically between 65-75°F (18-24°C) for most varieties. Use heating or cooling systems as needed to regulate indoor temperatures.
- **Humidity:** Control humidity levels to prevent mold and mildew growth, aiming for 50-60% humidity during the growing phase. Humidifiers or dehumidifiers can help adjust humidity levels as needed.
- **Lighting:** Provide adequate lighting for indoor growing using full-spectrum LED grow lights or natural sunlight supplemented with artificial lighting. Adjust lighting intensity and duration based on crop requirements and growth stages.

Example:
- **Location Example:** Suppose you are setting up a microgreens farm in an urban area with limited outdoor space. You decide to lease a warehouse space that offers easy access to transportation routes and utilities. You plan to convert the warehouse into an indoor growing facility equipped with climate control systems and LED grow lights to ensure year-round production and consistent crop quality.

Choosing the right location and determining space requirements are critical factors in setting up a successful microgreens farm. Whether opting for indoor or outdoor growing, consider climate and environmental controls to create optimal growing conditions for microgreen production. By carefully planning and implementing these factors, you can establish a thriving microgreens farm and meet the growing demand for fresh, nutritious greens in the market.

ESSENTIAL EQUIPMENT AND SUPPLIES

Seeds and Growing Mediums:
- **Seeds:** Select high-quality seeds specifically suited for microgreens production, such as broccoli, radish, or sunflower seeds. Purchase seeds from reputable suppliers to ensure germination rates and crop quality.
- **Growing Mediums:** Choose growing mediums like soilless potting mixes, coconut coir, or hydroponic mats, which provide optimal support and nutrition for microgreens growth.

Trays, Shelving, and Lighting:
- **Trays:** Invest in durable, food-safe trays suitable for microgreens production, such as plastic or recycled materials. Consider tray size and depth to accommodate different varieties and growing mediums.
- **Shelving:** Install sturdy shelving units to maximize vertical space and optimize growing area. Adjustable shelves allow for flexibility in arranging trays and accommodating different crop heights.
- **Lighting:** Provide adequate lighting for indoor growing using full-spectrum LED grow lights or natural sunlight supplemented with artificial lighting. Position lights at the appropriate distance and angle to ensure uniform coverage and optimal light intensity for photosynthesis.

Watering Systems and Tools:
- **Watering Systems:** Choose watering systems such as misting or drip irrigation systems to deliver water evenly and efficiently to microgreens trays. Automate watering schedules to maintain consistent moisture levels and minimize manual labor.
- **Tools:** Stock up on essential tools for microgreens cultivation, including hand sprayers, watering cans, scissors, and harvesting knives. Keep tools clean and sanitized to prevent contamination and maintain crop hygiene.

Setting Up Your Growing Area:
- **Designing Your Space:** Plan the layout of your growing area to maximize efficiency and workflow. Allocate space for growing, processing, and storage areas, and consider workflow patterns for easy movement and access.
- **Installing Equipment:** Install shelving units, lighting fixtures, and watering systems according to your design plan. Ensure proper assembly and secure installation to prevent accidents or damage during operation.
- **Ensuring Proper Ventilation and Light:** Provide adequate ventilation and air circulation to maintain optimal growing conditions and prevent humidity buildup and mold growth. Install exhaust fans or ventilation systems to remove stale air and regulate temperature and humidity levels. Position lighting fixtures to provide uniform coverage and adjust light intensity and duration based on crop requirements and growth stages.

Example:
- **Growing Area Example:** In your microgreens farm, you design a dedicated growing space in a climate-controlled warehouse equipped with shelving units and LED grow lights. You install misting irrigation systems and set

up automated watering schedules to ensure consistent moisture levels. Proper ventilation is ensured with exhaust fans and vents to maintain optimal airflow and prevent mold growth.

Equipping your microgreens farm with essential equipment and supplies is crucial for successful cultivation and production. By selecting high-quality seeds and growing mediums, investing in durable trays, shelving, and lighting, and implementing efficient watering systems and tools, you can create an optimal growing environment for microgreens production. Designing your growing area with proper ventilation and light ensures healthy and vigorous crop growth, leading to high-quality and nutritious microgreens for your customers.

GROWING MICROGREENS

Planting and Germination:

Seed Selection:
- Choose high-quality seeds specifically suited for microgreens production. Consider factors such as germination rate, flavor, and color variety.
- Experiment with different seed varieties to offer a diverse range of flavors and textures to your customers.

Sowing Techniques:
- Prepare growing trays or containers by filling them with a thin layer of moist growing medium.
- Scatter seeds evenly over the surface of the growing medium, aiming for a dense but not overcrowded distribution.
- Gently press the seeds into the growing medium to ensure good seed-to-soil contact for optimal germination.

Germination Methods:
- Cover the seeds with a thin layer of growing medium or a humidity dome to retain moisture and create a humid microclimate conducive to germination.
- Place the trays in a warm, well-lit area with indirect sunlight or under grow lights to encourage germination.
- Keep the growing medium consistently moist but not waterlogged to prevent mold growth and ensure

successful germination.

Caring for Your Microgreens:

Watering and Nutrients:

- Water microgreens regularly to maintain consistent moisture levels in the growing medium. Avoid overwatering, as it can lead to root rot and mold issues.
- Provide nutrients through the growing medium or use a diluted liquid fertilizer solution to supplement micronutrient requirements during the growing process.

Light Requirements:

- Ensure microgreens receive adequate light exposure for photosynthesis and healthy growth. Position trays near windows or under grow lights to provide sufficient light intensity.
- Adjust lighting duration and intensity based on crop requirements and growth stages, increasing light exposure as microgreens mature.

Pest and Disease Management:

- Monitor microgreens regularly for signs of pest infestation or disease, such as yellowing leaves, wilting, or discoloration.
- Practice good hygiene and sanitation practices to prevent the spread of pests and diseases, such as cleaning trays and tools between uses and removing any affected plants promptly.

Harvesting and Post-Harvest Handling:

When and How to Harvest:

- Harvest microgreens when they reach the desired size and stage of growth, typically 7-14 days after sowing, depending on the variety.
- Use clean, sharp scissors or harvesting knives to cut microgreens just above the soil line, leaving the roots intact for easier handling and packaging.

Cleaning and Packaging:
- Rinse harvested microgreens gently under cold running water to remove any soil or debris. Drain excess water and pat dry with paper towels or a clean kitchen towel.
- Package microgreens in clean, breathable containers or clamshells to maintain freshness and prevent wilting during storage and transportation.

Storing and Extending Shelf Life:
- Store harvested microgreens in the refrigerator at temperatures between 35-40°F (2-4°C) to extend shelf life and preserve quality.
- Use within 5-7 days for optimal freshness and flavor, or consider techniques such as vacuum sealing or controlled atmosphere storage to prolong shelf life.

Example:
- **Caring for Your Microgreens Example:** In your microgreens farm, you monitor seedlings daily for signs of germination and adjust watering and light levels as needed to promote healthy growth. You inspect trays regularly for pests and diseases, taking prompt action to mitigate any issues and ensure optimal crop health.

Growing microgreens requires attention to detail and care throughout the entire process, from planting and germination to harvesting and post-harvest handling. By selecting high-quality seeds, providing proper care and maintenance, and implementing effective harvesting and storage techniques, you can produce fresh, nutritious microgreens with vibrant colors and flavors for your customers to enjoy.

MARKETING AND SELLING MICROGREENS

Creating Your Brand:
Brand Identity and Logo:
- Define your brand identity by identifying your mission, values, and unique selling propositions (USPs).
- Design a logo and brand visuals that reflect your brand identity and resonate with your target audience.

Packaging and Labeling:
- Choose packaging materials and designs that showcase the freshness and quality of your microgreens.
- Include clear and informative labels with product details, nutritional information, and branding elements.

Developing a Website and Online Presence:
- Create a professional website to showcase your products, share your story, and engage with customers online.
- Utilize social media platforms and online marketplaces to expand your reach and connect with potential customers.

Sales Channels and Strategies:
Selling Direct to Consumers:
- Offer online ordering and delivery services to reach consumers directly.
- Participate in local farmers' markets or community

events to engage with customers in person and build brand awareness.

Partnering with Restaurants and Grocery Stores:
- Establish partnerships with local restaurants, cafes, and grocery stores to supply fresh microgreens for their menus or shelves.
- Provide samples and conduct product demonstrations to showcase the quality and versatility of your microgreens to potential partners.

Farmers' Markets and CSA Programs:
- Participate in farmers' markets or community-supported agriculture (CSA) programs to sell directly to consumers and build relationships with local communities.
- Offer subscription-based CSA programs to provide customers with regular deliveries of fresh microgreens.

Pricing and Profitability:

Pricing Strategies:
- Determine pricing strategies based on market demand, competition, and production costs.
- Consider factors such as seasonality, variety, and packaging size when setting prices for your microgreens.

Cost Analysis and Margins:
- Conduct a thorough cost analysis to determine the true cost of producing microgreens, including seed costs, growing supplies, labor, and overhead expenses.
- Calculate profit margins and adjust pricing as needed to ensure profitability while remaining competitive in the market.

Maximizing Profitability:
- Explore opportunities to reduce production costs through efficient farming practices, bulk purchasing, or automation.
- Continuously monitor sales performance and customer

feedback to identify areas for improvement and maximize profitability.

Example:
- **Sales Channels Example:** You launch an online store and social media accounts to promote your microgreens brand and attract customers. You partner with local restaurants and grocery stores to supply fresh microgreens for their menus and shelves, while also participating in farmers' markets on weekends to sell directly to consumers.

Conclusion:
Effective marketing and sales strategies are essential for successfully promoting and selling microgreens. By creating a strong brand identity, developing a professional online presence, and exploring various sales channels and pricing strategies, you can reach a wider audience, build customer loyalty, and maximize profitability in the competitive microgreens market. Regularly evaluate and adjust your marketing and sales efforts to adapt to changing market conditions and meet the evolving needs of your customers.

SCALING UP YOUR MICROGREENS BUSINESS

Expanding Production:
Increasing Growing Capacity:
- Evaluate your current growing capacity and infrastructure to identify opportunities for expansion.
- Invest in additional growing equipment, such as shelving units, lighting, and irrigation systems, to increase production volume.

Adding New Varieties:
- Research and introduce new microgreens varieties to diversify your product offerings and appeal to a wider range of customers.
- Experiment with different seed suppliers and growing techniques to expand your repertoire of microgreens varieties.

Optimizing Production Efficiency:
- Streamline production processes and workflows to minimize waste and maximize efficiency.
- Implement automation and technology solutions, such as automated watering systems or inventory management software, to improve productivity and reduce labor costs.

Diversifying Your Product Line:

Value-Added Products:
- Explore opportunities to create value-added products using microgreens, such as pre-packaged salads, smoothie blends, or gourmet spice blends.
- Package microgreens with complementary ingredients or recipe cards to provide added convenience and value to customers.

Offering Kits and Educational Workshops:
- Develop microgreens growing kits or DIY starter packs for customers interested in growing their own microgreens at home.
- Host educational workshops or online tutorials to teach customers about microgreens cultivation and culinary uses, building engagement and loyalty.

Subscription Services:
- Launch subscription-based services, such as weekly or monthly microgreens deliveries, to provide customers with a convenient and consistent supply of fresh greens.
- Offer customizable subscription plans based on customer preferences and dietary needs.

Building a Team:

Hiring Employees:
- Assess your staffing needs and recruit qualified candidates to fill key roles in production, sales, and administration.
- Seek individuals with relevant experience or a passion for sustainable agriculture and healthy living to align with your business values.

Training and Management:
- Provide comprehensive training and ongoing support to your team members to ensure they have the necessary skills and knowledge to perform their roles effectively.
- Foster a positive work culture and encourage

open communication and collaboration among team members.

Outsourcing and Partnerships:
- Consider outsourcing certain tasks or services, such as marketing or distribution, to specialized agencies or partners to leverage their expertise and resources.
- Establish strategic partnerships with local suppliers, distributors, or retailers to expand your market reach and distribution channels.

Example:
- **Scaling Up Example:** You decide to expand your microgreens business by investing in additional growing equipment and infrastructure to double your production capacity. You introduce several new microgreens varieties and launch a subscription service offering weekly microgreens deliveries to customers. To support your growing operations, you hire additional staff members and implement training programs to ensure they are equipped to handle increased demand.

Conclusion:
Scaling up your microgreens business requires careful planning and execution to sustain growth while maintaining product quality and customer satisfaction. By expanding production capacity, diversifying your product line, building a talented team, and optimizing production efficiency, you can position your business for long-term success and capitalize on opportunities for growth in the dynamic microgreens market. Regularly assess your progress and adapt your strategies as needed to stay agile and responsive to changing market conditions and customer preferences.

CASE STUDIES AND SUCCESS STORIES IN MICROGREENS BUSINESS

Inspirational Case Studies:
Profiles of Successful Microgreens Businesses:

- Explore case studies of established microgreens businesses that have achieved success in the industry.
- Highlight the stories of entrepreneurs who have built thriving microgreens farms, developed innovative products, and created strong brands.

Key Takeaways and Lessons Learned:
Lessons in Business Growth:

- Analyze the strategies and tactics employed by successful microgreens businesses to scale up their operations and expand their market reach.
- Identify key success factors, such as product differentiation, customer engagement, and operational efficiency.

Overcoming Challenges:
Common Obstacles and Solutions:

- Examine common challenges faced by microgreens businesses, such as seasonal fluctuations in demand, production constraints, and competition.

- Discuss effective solutions and strategies for mitigating challenges, such as diversifying product offerings, optimizing production processes, and implementing marketing initiatives.

Adapting to Market Changes:
- Discuss how successful microgreens businesses have adapted to changes in consumer preferences, market trends, and regulatory requirements.
- Highlight examples of businesses that have successfully pivoted their strategies in response to emerging opportunities or challenges.

Staying Resilient and Innovative:

Cultivating Resilience:
- Showcase examples of microgreens businesses that have demonstrated resilience in the face of adversity, such as natural disasters, supply chain disruptions, or economic downturns.
- Discuss resilience-building strategies, such as financial planning, diversification, and community engagement.

Fostering Innovation:
- Explore how successful microgreens businesses have fostered innovation in product development, marketing, and sustainability practices.
- Highlight examples of businesses that have embraced technological advancements, adopted sustainable farming practices, or launched innovative product lines.

Example:
- **Success Story Example:** Green Sprout Farms, a family-owned microgreens farm, started as a small operation in a backyard greenhouse. Through strategic partnerships with local restaurants and farmers' markets, they expanded their customer base and grew their business. Despite facing challenges such as weather fluctuations

and supply chain disruptions, they remained resilient and innovative, experimenting with new growing techniques and introducing value-added products like microgreens salad mixes. Today, Green Sprout Farms is a leading supplier of fresh microgreens in their region, known for their commitment to quality, sustainability, and community engagement.

Conclusion:

Case studies and success stories of microgreens businesses offer valuable insights and inspiration for aspiring entrepreneurs in the industry. By examining the experiences of successful businesses, identifying key lessons learned, and learning how to overcome challenges and stay resilient and innovative, you can apply these insights to your own microgreens venture and set yourself up for success in the dynamic and competitive market. Continuously seek opportunities for learning and growth, and be open to adapting your strategies in response to changing market conditions and customer needs.

FUTURE TRENDS AND OPPORTUNITIES IN MICROGREENS BUSINESS

Emerging Trends in Microgreens:
Health and Wellness:
- Discuss the growing consumer demand for fresh, nutritious foods and the role of microgreens in promoting health and wellness.
- Highlight the nutritional benefits of microgreens, such as high levels of vitamins, minerals, and antioxidants, and their potential contribution to a healthy diet.

Sustainable and Organic Farming:
- Explore the increasing emphasis on sustainable and organic farming practices in the agriculture industry.
- Discuss the benefits of microgreens cultivation for sustainable food production, including reduced water usage, carbon footprint, and environmental impact.

Technological Innovations:
- Examine technological advancements in microgreens farming, such as hydroponic and vertical farming systems, automated growing equipment, and precision agriculture techniques.
- Discuss the potential of technology to improve efficiency,

productivity, and resource management in microgreens production.

Exploring New Markets:

Expanding Geographically:
- Identify opportunities for geographical expansion in underserved or emerging markets, both locally and internationally.
- Discuss strategies for entering new markets, such as conducting market research, building local partnerships, and adapting products to meet regional preferences.

Tapping into Institutional Markets:
- Explore opportunities for supplying microgreens to institutional markets, such as restaurants, hotels, schools, and healthcare facilities.
- Discuss the benefits of forming partnerships with institutional buyers and meeting their demand for fresh, locally sourced produce.

Exporting and Global Opportunities:
- Assess the potential for exporting microgreens to international markets and tapping into global demand for fresh, high-quality produce.
- Discuss considerations for entering foreign markets, such as regulatory requirements, logistics, and cultural preferences.

Example:
- **Future Trend Example:** GreenTech Farms, a leading microgreens producer, is embracing technological innovations to enhance sustainability and efficiency in their operations. They have implemented vertical farming systems and automated growing equipment to maximize space utilization and reduce resource consumption. Additionally, they are exploring new markets for geographical expansion, targeting urban areas with high demand for fresh, locally grown

produce. By combining technological advancements with strategic market expansion, GreenTech Farms is poised for continued growth and success in the evolving microgreens industry.

Conclusion:

The future of the microgreens industry holds promising opportunities for growth and innovation. By staying informed about emerging trends such as health and wellness, sustainable farming practices, technological innovations, and exploring new markets for geographical expansion and institutional partnerships, microgreens businesses can position themselves for success in the dynamic and competitive market. Continuously adapt to changing consumer preferences and market dynamics, and leverage technological advancements to drive efficiency and sustainability in your operations. By embracing these future trends and opportunities, you can build a resilient and thriving microgreens business that meets the evolving needs of customers and contributes to a healthier and more sustainable food system.

RESOURCES AND TOOLS FOR MICROGREENS BUSINESS

Essential Resources:

Seed Suppliers and Equipment Vendors:
- Research and compile a list of reputable seed suppliers and equipment vendors specializing in microgreens cultivation.
- Evaluate factors such as seed quality, variety selection, pricing, and customer service when choosing suppliers for seeds, trays, lighting, and other growing equipment.

Marketing and Sales Platforms:
- Explore marketing and sales platforms to promote and sell your microgreens, such as e-commerce websites, social media platforms, and online marketplaces.
- Consider utilizing specialized platforms for farmers and food producers, as well as local farmers' markets and community-supported agriculture (CSA) programs.

Educational and Networking Resources:
- Seek out educational resources and networking opportunities to learn more about microgreens cultivation, business management, and industry trends.
- Join online forums, attend workshops or conferences,

and connect with other microgreens growers and industry professionals for knowledge sharing and collaboration.

Appendix:

Sample Business Plan:

- Provide a sample business plan template tailored specifically for microgreens businesses, including sections on executive summary, market analysis, marketing and sales strategies, operations, and financial projections.
- Use the sample business plan as a guide for developing your own customized business plan for your microgreens venture.

Checklist for Starting Your Microgreens Business:

- Create a checklist outlining the essential steps and considerations for starting a microgreens business, from securing permits and licenses to setting up growing infrastructure and developing marketing strategies.
- Use the checklist to ensure you cover all the necessary aspects of starting your microgreens business and stay organized throughout the process.

Glossary of Terms:

- Compile a glossary of key terms and terminology commonly used in microgreens cultivation and business management.
- Include definitions and explanations for terms related to growing techniques, plant biology, marketing, sales, and finance to serve as a reference for beginners and experienced growers alike.

Example:

- **Resource Example:** GreenThumb Co. provides a comprehensive list of seed suppliers, equipment vendors, and marketing platforms in their resource guide for microgreens growers. They also offer educational webinars and networking events for members to learn from industry experts and connect with other growers. Additionally, GreenThumb Co. provides a sample business plan template and checklist for starting a microgreens business, along with a glossary of terms to help growers navigate the industry with confidence.

Conclusion:

Access to essential resources and tools is crucial for starting and growing a successful microgreens business. By leveraging reputable seed suppliers, equipment vendors, marketing platforms, and educational resources, as well as utilizing sample business plans, checklists, and glossaries for reference, microgreens entrepreneurs can build a strong foundation for their ventures and navigate the complexities of the industry with confidence. Continuously seek out new resources and stay informed about industry developments to stay competitive and innovative in the dynamic microgreens market.

YOUR JOURNEY IN MICROGREENS

Congratulations on completing this comprehensive guide to starting and growing a successful microgreens business! Throughout this journey, you've gained valuable insights into the world of microgreens cultivation, business management, and industry trends. As you embark on your microgreens venture, let's recap the key points covered and offer some encouragement and motivation for your future growth.

Recap of Key Points:

- **Understanding Microgreens:** You've learned about the basics of microgreens, including their nutritional benefits, growing techniques, and culinary uses.
- **Starting Your Business:** We've explored essential steps for starting a microgreens business, from planning and setup to marketing and sales.
- **Scaling Up and Future Trends:** You've discovered strategies for scaling up your business and exploring future trends and opportunities in the microgreens industry.

Encouragement and Motivation:

Starting and growing a microgreens business can be a rewarding journey filled with challenges and successes. Remember to stay focused on your goals, maintain a positive mindset, and embrace opportunities for learning and growth along the way. Celebrate your achievements, no matter how small, and learn from setbacks to become stronger and more resilient.

Next Steps and Future Growth:

As you move forward with your microgreens business, continue to refine your skills, expand your knowledge, and adapt to evolving market trends. Keep exploring new varieties, experimenting with growing techniques, and innovating in your products and services. Network with other growers, seek mentorship, and stay connected to the microgreens community to share experiences and support each other's growth.

Conclusion:

Your journey in microgreens is just beginning, and the possibilities for success are endless. With dedication, passion, and perseverance, you can build a thriving microgreens business that not only sustains you financially but also contributes to a healthier and more sustainable food system. Keep dreaming big, stay inspired, and never lose sight of the impact you can make in the world through your passion for microgreens.

Best of luck on your microgreens journey, and may your business flourish and thrive in the years to come!

CASE STUDY 1: HAMAMA

Overview: Hamama is a well-known microgreens company that specializes in home-growing kits for microgreens.

Initial Investment:
- The founders, Camille Rich and Daniel Goodman, started Hamama with an initial investment of around $200,000, which included costs for research and development, prototype creation, and initial marketing efforts.

Current Revenue:
- As of the latest available information, Hamama's annual revenue is estimated to be in the millions of dollars. The exact figure fluctuates, but in 2021, their revenue was reported to be over $3 million.

Key Strategies:
- **Product Innovation:** Hamama developed a unique growing kit that simplifies the process of growing microgreens at home.
- **E-commerce Focus:** They leveraged online sales through their website and platforms like Amazon.
- **Subscription Model:** They offer a subscription service for regular delivery of microgreen seed quilts.

CASE STUDY 2: THE CHEF'S GARDEN

Overview: The Chef's Garden is a family-owned farm in Ohio that provides specialty microgreens, herbs, and vegetables to top chefs and restaurants across the country.

Initial Investment:
- The Jones family, who run The Chef's Garden, invested significant capital in acquiring and developing their farm. Exact initial investment details are not publicly disclosed, but developing a commercial farm can cost several hundred thousand dollars to a few million.

Current Revenue:
- The Chef's Garden generates millions in annual revenue, with a diverse product range that includes microgreens. The exact revenue from microgreens alone is part of their broader income, but the business is a multi-million dollar operation.

Key Strategies:
- **Direct Marketing to Chefs:** Building relationships with top chefs and restaurants.
- **Educational Initiatives:** Hosting events and educational programs to teach about sustainable farming.
- **Quality and Diversity:** Offering a wide variety of high-quality, specialty produce.

CASE STUDY 3: TINY GREENS

Overview: Tiny Greens is a small-scale microgreens business based in Illinois, focusing on local markets and online sales.

Initial Investment:
- The founders started with an investment of about $10,000, covering costs for seeds, trays, grow lights, and initial marketing efforts.

Current Revenue:
- Tiny Greens generates an estimated annual revenue of around $100,000 to $150,000. This is a rough estimate based on the scale of their operations and sales channels.

Key Strategies:
- **Local Farmers' Markets:** Building a loyal customer base through regular attendance at farmers' markets.
- **Online Sales:** Expanding reach through a well-designed website and social media marketing.
- **Partnerships:** Collaborating with local health food stores and restaurants.

CASE STUDY 4: CITY ROOTS

Overview: City Roots is an urban farm in Columbia, South Carolina, that produces microgreens, mushrooms, and other organic produce.

Initial Investment:
- City Roots started with an initial investment of around $50,000, which included the cost of land, infrastructure, and initial supplies.

Current Revenue:
- City Roots has grown to generate approximately $500,000 in annual revenue, with microgreens being a significant part of their product line.

Key Strategies:
- **Urban Farming:** Utilizing urban spaces to grow fresh, organic produce.
- **CSA Programs:** Offering Community Supported Agriculture (CSA) programs to provide regular produce to subscribers.
- **Education and Events:** Hosting workshops and farm tours to engage with the community.

KEY TAKEAWAYS FROM CASE STUDIES:

1. **Initial Investment:** Varies widely from as low as $10,000 for small-scale operations to several hundred thousand dollars for larger, more diversified farms.
2. **Revenue Potential:** Can range from $100,000 for small businesses to millions for well-established operations.
3. **Sales Channels:** Direct sales to consumers (farmers' markets, online), partnerships with local restaurants and grocery stores, and subscription services.
4. **Marketing Strategies:** Leveraging online platforms, building local relationships, and focusing on product quality and diversity.
5. **Scaling Up:** Successful businesses often start small and scale up by reinvesting profits, expanding product lines, and increasing production capacity.

ADDITIONAL RESOURCES:

- **Seed Companies:** Johnny's Selected Seeds, True Leaf Market
- **Supplies and Equipment:** Bootstrap Farmer, Gardener's Supply Company

Below is a detailed guide on how to grow each of the popular microgreen varieties, including the suitable season for growth, growth time, and shelf life.

1. RADISH MICROGREENS

- **How to Grow:**
    - Soak seeds for 6-8 hours.
    - Spread seeds evenly on moistened growing medium.
    - Cover with another tray or a humidity dome for 2-3 days until germination.
    - Expose to light and water daily.
- **Suitable Season:** Year-round.
- **Growth Time:** 6-10 days.
- **Shelf Life:** 5-7 days in the refrigerator.

2. SUNFLOWER MICROGREENS

- **How to Grow:**
    - Soak seeds for 8-12 hours.
    - Spread seeds on moistened growing medium.
    - Cover with a tray for 2-3 days until germination.
    - Provide ample light and water daily.
- **Suitable Season:** Year-round.
- **Growth Time:** 7-14 days.
- **Shelf Life:** 5-7 days in the refrigerator.

3. PEA SHOOTS

- **How to Grow:**
    - Soak seeds for 8-12 hours.
    - Spread seeds on a moistened growing medium.
    - Cover with a tray for 3-4 days until germination.
    - Provide light and water daily.
- **Suitable Season:** Year-round.
- **Growth Time:** 10-14 days.
- **Shelf Life:** 5-7 days in the refrigerator.

4. BROCCOLI MICROGREENS

- **How to Grow:**
  - Spread seeds on moistened growing medium.
  - Cover with a tray or dome for 2-3 days until germination.
  - Provide light and water daily.
- **Suitable Season:** Year-round.
- **Growth Time:** 10-14 days.
- **Shelf Life:** 5-7 days in the refrigerator.

5. BASIL MICROGREENS

- **How to Grow:**
    - Spread seeds on moistened growing medium.
    - Cover with a humidity dome for 3-4 days until germination.
    - Provide light and water daily.
- **Suitable Season:** Spring and summer.
- **Growth Time:** 12-21 days.
- **Shelf Life:** 5-7 days in the refrigerator.

6. ARUGULA MICROGREENS

- **How to Grow:**
    - Spread seeds on moistened growing medium.
    - Cover with a tray for 2-3 days until germination.
    - Provide light and water daily.
- **Suitable Season:** Year-round.
- **Growth Time:** 10-14 days.
- **Shelf Life:** 5-7 days in the refrigerator.

7. CILANTRO MICROGREENS

- **How to Grow:**
  - Spread seeds on moistened growing medium.
  - Cover with a tray or dome for 3-4 days until germination.
  - Provide light and water daily.
- **Suitable Season:** Spring and fall.
- **Growth Time:** 10-14 days.
- **Shelf Life:** 5-7 days in the refrigerator.

8. KALE MICROGREENS

- **How to Grow:**
    - Spread seeds on moistened growing medium.
    - Cover with a tray for 2-3 days until germination.
    - Provide light and water daily.
- **Suitable Season:** Year-round.
- **Growth Time:** 8-12 days.
- **Shelf Life:** 5-7 days in the refrigerator.

9. MUSTARD MICROGREENS

- **How to Grow:**
    - Spread seeds on moistened growing medium.
    - Cover with a tray for 2-3 days until germination.
    - Provide light and water daily.
- **Suitable Season:** Year-round.
- **Growth Time:** 6-10 days.
- **Shelf Life:** 5-7 days in the refrigerator.

10. BEET MICROGREENS

- **How to Grow:**
    - Spread seeds on moistened growing medium.
    - Cover with a tray for 3-4 days until germination.
    - Provide light and water daily.
- **Suitable Season:** Year-round.
- **Growth Time:** 10-14 days.
- **Shelf Life:** 5-7 days in the refrigerator.

11. SWISS CHARD MICROGREENS

- **How to Grow:**
    - Spread seeds on moistened growing medium.
    - Cover with a tray for 3-4 days until germination.
    - Provide light and water daily.
- **Suitable Season:** Year-round.
- **Growth Time:** 10-14 days.
- **Shelf Life:** 5-7 days in the refrigerator.

12. SPINACH MICROGREENS

- **How to Grow:**
    - Spread seeds on moistened growing medium.
    - Cover with a tray for 3-4 days until germination.
    - Provide light and water daily.
- **Suitable Season:** Spring and fall.
- **Growth Time:** 10-14 days.
- **Shelf Life:** 5-7 days in the refrigerator.

13. AMARANTH MICROGREENS

- **How to Grow:**
    - Spread seeds on moistened growing medium.
    - Cover with a tray for 2-3 days until germination.
    - Provide light and water daily.
- **Suitable Season:** Year-round.
- **Growth Time:** 8-12 days.
- **Shelf Life:** 5-7 days in the refrigerator.

14. FENUGREEK MICROGREENS

- **How to Grow:**
  - Spread seeds on moistened growing medium.
  - Cover with a tray for 2-3 days until germination.
  - Provide light and water daily.
- **Suitable Season:** Year-round.
- **Growth Time:** 8-12 days.
- **Shelf Life:** 5-7 days in the refrigerator.

15. WHEATGRASS

- **How to Grow:**
    - Soak seeds for 8-12 hours.
    - Spread seeds on moistened growing medium.
    - Cover with a tray for 2-3 days until germination.
    - Provide light and water daily.
- **Suitable Season:** Year-round.
- **Growth Time:** 7-10 days.
- **Shelf Life:** 5-7 days in the refrigerator.

IMPORTANT CONSIDERATIONS FOR BUSINESS:

- **Lighting:** Ensure adequate lighting, using grow lights if natural light is insufficient.
- **Watering:** Maintain consistent moisture, avoiding overwatering to prevent mold.
- **Temperature and Humidity:** Ideal growing conditions are typically between 60-75°F (15-24°C) with 40-60% humidity.
- **Hygiene:** Maintain cleanliness to avoid contamination and ensure food safety.
- **Market Demand:** Tailor your crop choices to local market preferences and demands.
- **Storage:** Microgreens are best stored in the refrigerator in sealed containers to maintain freshness.
- **Scaling:** Start small and scale up as you gain experience and market share.

A SAMPLE LIST OF SOME COMMON MICROGREENS VARIETIES AND THEIR USES:

Broccoli Microgreens:
    Uses: Salads, sandwiches, garnishes.
    Nutritional Value: High in vitamins A, C, and K, as well as antioxidants.

Radish Microgreens:
    Uses: Sandwiches, wraps, tacos.
    Nutritional Value: Rich in vitamin C, fiber, and potassium.

Pea Shoots:
    Uses: Stir-fries, soups, smoothies.
    Nutritional Value: Excellent source of protein, fiber, and vitamins A and C.

Sunflower Microgreens:
    Uses: Salads, grain bowls, pesto.
    Nutritional Value: High in vitamin E, magnesium, and selenium.

Arugula Microgreens:
    Uses: Pizza toppings, pasta dishes, omelets.

Nutritional Value: Rich in vitamin K, calcium, and iron.

Cilantro Microgreens:

Uses: Mexican dishes, salsas, guacamole.

Nutritional Value: Good source of vitamin A, vitamin C, and antioxidants.

Beet Microgreens:

Uses: Smoothies, salads, soups.

Nutritional Value: High in folate, manganese, and betalains.

Kale Microgreens:

Uses: Smoothies, sandwiches, wraps.

Nutritional Value: Rich in vitamins A, C, and K, as well as calcium and iron.

Basil Microgreens:

Uses: Pasta dishes, pizzas, bruschetta.

Nutritional Value: High in vitamin K, iron, and antioxidants.

Mustard Microgreens:

Uses: Sandwiches, burgers, pickles.

Nutritional Value: Rich in vitamins A, C, and K, as well as calcium and magnesium.

Chia Microgreens:

Uses: Smoothie bowls, puddings, salads.

Nutritional Value: High in omega-3 fatty acids, protein, and fiber.

Amaranth Microgreens:

Uses: Stir-fries, curries, soups.

Nutritional Value: Rich in iron, calcium, and protein.

Cabbage Microgreens:

Uses: Tacos, coleslaw, sandwiches.

Nutritional Value: High in vitamin C, fiber, and antioxidants.

Garlic Microgreens:

Uses: Pasta dishes, marinades, soups.

Nutritional Value: Contains allicin, a compound with potential health benefits.

Fennel Microgreens:

Uses: Seafood dishes, salads, garnishes.

Nutritional Value: Rich in fiber, vitamin C, and antioxidants.

Mizuna Microgreens:

Uses: Asian stir-fries, salads, sushi rolls.

Nutritional Value: High in vitamins A, C, and K, as well as iron and calcium.

Red Amaranth Microgreens:

Uses: Salads, wraps, smoothies.

Nutritional Value: Rich in antioxidants, vitamins, and minerals.

Borage Microgreens:

Uses: Salads, cocktails, desserts.

Nutritional Value: High in gamma-linolenic acid (GLA) and other beneficial compounds.

Shiso Microgreens:

Uses: Sushi, salads, garnishes.

Nutritional Value: Contains antioxidants and aromatic compounds with potential health benefits.

Sorrel Microgreens:

Uses: Soups, salads, sauces.

Nutritional Value: High in vitamins A and C, and minerals like potassium and magnesium.

Watercress Microgreens:

Uses: Sandwiches, salads, garnishes.

Nutritional Value: Rich in vitamins K, C, and antioxidants like beta-carotene.

Shungiku Microgreens:

Uses: Asian stir-fries, hot pot, soups.

Nutritional Value: High in vitamins A, C, and calcium.

Lettuce Microgreens:

Uses: Salads, sandwiches, wraps.

Nutritional Value: Contains vitamins A, K, and folate, as well as antioxidants.

Okra Microgreens:

Uses: Stir-fries, curries, soups.

Nutritional Value: Rich in fiber, vitamins C and K, and minerals like calcium and magnesium.

Savory Microgreens:

Uses: Meat dishes, stuffing, salads.

Nutritional Value: Contains essential oils and antioxidants.

Chard Microgreens:

Uses: Smoothies, salads, sautés.

Nutritional Value: High in vitamins A, C, and K, as well as magnesium and potassium.

Kohlrabi Microgreens:

Uses: Salads, slaws, stir-fries.

Nutritional Value: Rich in vitamins C and K, and minerals like potassium and manganese.

Chicory Microgreens:

Uses: Salads, sandwiches, garnishes.

Nutritional Value: Contains inulin, a prebiotic fiber, and antioxidants.

Dill Microgreens:

Uses: Seafood dishes, salads, sauces.

Nutritional Value: Rich in vitamins A, C, and minerals like calcium and iron.

Celery Microgreens:

Uses: Salads, soups, smoothies.

Nutritional Value: High in vitamins A, C, and K, and minerals like potassium and folate.

Parsley Microgreens:

Uses: Garnishes, salads, soups.

Nutritional Value: Rich in vitamins A, C, and K, and minerals like iron and calcium.

Basil Microgreens:

Uses: Pasta dishes, pizzas, pesto.

Nutritional Value: High in vitamin K, iron, and antioxidants.

Coriander Microgreens:

Uses: Indian dishes, chutneys, salads.

Nutritional Value: Contains antioxidants, vitamins, and minerals like iron and manganese.

Chervil Microgreens:

Uses: French cuisine, soups, salads.

Nutritional Value: Rich in vitamins A and C, and minerals like calcium and potassium.

Lemon Balm Microgreens:

Uses: Tea infusions, desserts, salads.

Nutritional Value: Contains essential oils and antioxidants.

Oregano Microgreens:

Uses: Italian dishes, sauces, marinades.

Nutritional Value: Rich in antioxidants and aromatic compounds.

Tarragon Microgreens:

Uses: Chicken dishes, sauces, salads.

Nutritional Value: Contains essential oils and antioxidants.

Mint Microgreens:

Uses: Cocktails, desserts, salads.

Nutritional Value: Refreshing flavor and potential digestive benefits.

Lavender Microgreens:

Uses: Baking, teas, desserts.

Nutritional Value: Aromatic flavor and potential calming effects.

Lemongrass Microgreens:

Uses: Asian dishes, teas, soups.

Nutritional Value: Citrusy flavor and potential anti-inflammatory properties.

Marjoram Microgreens:

Uses: Mediterranean dishes, soups, salads.

Nutritional Value: Aromatic flavor and potential digestive benefits.

Chive Microgreens:

Uses: Garnishes, salads, omelets.

Nutritional Value: Mild onion flavor and potential digestive benefits.

Sage Microgreens:

Uses: Meat dishes, stuffing, teas.

Nutritional Value: Aromatic flavor and potential cognitive benefits.

Thyme Microgreens:

Uses: Roasted vegetables, soups, sauces.

Nutritional Value: Aromatic flavor and potential respiratory benefits.

Cress Microgreens:

Uses: Sandwiches, salads, garnishes.

Nutritional Value: Peppery flavor and high in vitamins and minerals.

.

LASKAR

www.ingramcontent.com/pod-product-compliance
Lightning Source LLC
Chambersburg PA
CBHW050236230526
45470CB00005B/1974